COMMANDING SUCCESS

Unveiling the Ultimate Secrets of
Successful Leadership

Franklin J. Perry

Copyright © 2023 by Franklin J. Perry

All rights reserved.

No part of this publication may be reproduced, distributed, or transmitted in any form or by any means, including photocopying, recording, or other electronic or mechanical methods, without the prior written permission of the publisher, except in the case of brief quotations embodied in critical reviews and certain other noncommercial uses permitted by copyright law.

Book Cover by Ziovil Media

Acknowledgments

To my incredible support system: my family, friends, and loved ones. Your unwavering belief in me and your encouragement kept me going. Thank you for being my guiding light.

To the experts and mentors who generously shared their knowledge and wisdom, shaping the ideas within these pages, I am forever grateful. Your insights have enriched this book beyond measure.

To my editor and the dedicated team at Ziovil Media, thank you for your expertise and dedication in helping me refine this work into its best version.

And to you, dear reader, thank you for joining me on this journey. Your presence and support mean the world to me.

With heartfelt appreciation,

Contents

Acknowledgments

INTRODUCTION

Secret 1
REGENERATION

Secrete 2
KNOW YOUR FOLLOWERS

Secret 3
INDISPENSABILITY

Secrete 4
UNIQUENESS

Secrete5
BE ATTRACTIVE

Secrete 6
RESILIENCE

Take Home Note

INTRODUCTION

Sometime in the distant past in a land controlled by lords and sovereigns, a youthful and aggressive ruler named Alexander set out on a hazardous journey to reveal the mysteries behind powerful leadership. Not entirely settled to transcend the requirements of his inheritance and become a genuine expert of impact, he looked for the direction of a shrewd old sage known as Lord Greene.

Settled profound inside the charming woods, Lord Greene lived in a modest bungalow, encompassed by old books and the murmurs of shrewdness went down through ages. The ruler moved toward the wise, his eyes sparkling with interest and a voracious crave information.

"Sir Greene," Alexander said, "I long to figure out the purpose of leadership. I wish to figure out how to explore the misleading waters of impact and transcend the common. Could you at any point direct me on this way?"

The old sage grinned, his eyes gleaming with a mix of underhandedness and smarts. He coaxed the ruler to sit by the chimney, where the blazes moved and snapped, providing reason to feel ambiguous about an ethereal sparkle the room.

"Ok, youthful ruler, you have set out upon an excursion that numerous before you have looked for," Greene started. "The way to leadership is both many-sided and hazardous, yet with the right information and understanding, you can shape your fate."

With a shine of energy in his eyes, the young ruler Alexander inclined forward, anxious to retain the savvy's insight.

Thus, Greene started to wind around an embroidery of stories from far off terrains and past periods. He recapped the story of a finesse retainer who became the best at inconspicuous blandishment, acquiring the blessing of the ruler without exciting doubt. Through this story, Alexander took in the significance of never eclipsing those in, influential places and the craft of vital lowliness.

In another story, Greene disclosed the narrative of a strong conqueror who grasped the power of eccentricity. By keeping his enemies in a condition of ceaseless tension, he amplified his own impact and struck dread into the hearts of his opponents.

This story enlightened the benefit of developing a quality of secret and the cautious sending of force.

As the days transformed into weeks, Alexander listened eagerly, absorbing the insight of the sage. He found that power was not exclusively about power and control however about grasping the hearts and psyches of others. Ace Greene showed him the specialty of sympathy, the meaning of perceiving individuals' longings and fears, and the force of utilizing these experiences to manufacture unions and gain impact.

Over the course of their time together, Greene disclosed every one of the secretes that makes successful leaders of the world, each a string in the terrific embroidery of human instinct and impact. The ruler figured out how to cover his expectations, to express not exactly essential, and to adjust to consistently evolving conditions.

Yet, as the ruler drove further into the lessons, an acknowledgment unfolded upon him. These regulations were not simply devices for control and predominance. They were likewise mirroring the intricacies of human association, asking him to scrutinize his own intentions and the results of his activities.

Directed by Greene's insight, Alexander found that genuine dominance of leadership was not accomplished through blind desire but rather through mindfulness and uprightness. The rules were not orders to be understood without thought yet standards to be perceived, dissected, and applied with intelligence and insight.

Thus, equipped with the information and experiences acquired from his experiences with old Greene, Alexander got back to his realm. He turned into a pioneer known for his empathy, vital reasoning, and capacity to move others to significance. He comprehended that power was not an end in itself but rather a way to make positive change and elevate people around him.

What's more, presently, dear reader, it is your chance to set out on this groundbreaking excursion through the pages of "Commanding Success." The stories and lessons of Greene are not bound to the domain of old times and respectable courts; they are immortal rules that resound in our advanced world.

Whether you are a sprouting business visionary, an understudy trying to explore the intricacies of social elements, or a pioneer endeavoring to have an enduring effect, the insight inside these pages holds colossal worth. An aide can engage you to explore the perplexing snare of impact, discussion, and self-improvement.

As you dig into every regulation, stop and reflect. Consider how these standards cross with your own encounters, goals, and collaborations. Embrace the information not as an outline for misleading and control, but rather as a significant comprehension of the complexities of force elements. It is through this understanding that you can outline your own way with uprightness and legitimacy.

Apply the examples to your own and proficient life, however consistently recall the moral obligation that accompanies power. Let your quest for power be directed by a certifiable craving to elevate others, encourage significant associations, and make positive change. Utilize these regulations not as weapons but rather as devices to explore the intricacies of human collaboration with intelligence, empathy, and regard.

In reality as we know it, power elements shape our connections, choices, and desires, "Commanding Success" fills in as a signal of understanding and direction. By embracing the standards inside these pages, you can hoist yourself, comprehend others all the more profoundly, and have an enduring effect.

Presently, venture out on this extraordinary journey. Open the book, submerge yourself in its insight, and let the secretes of leadership enlighten your way. Furnish yourself with the information, understanding, and mindfulness to explore the intricacies of our reality, and may your quest for power be directed by the standards of honesty, sympathy, and a longing to elevate and motivate everyone around you.

Your predetermination anticipates, and inside " Commanding Success," you will track down the keys to open your actual potential.

Secret

REGENERATION

Life is a journey of constant growth and change. As we navigate the complexities of the world, we often find ourselves faced with challenges, setbacks, and moments of stagnation. In these moments, the concept of recreating oneself becomes both a powerful opportunity and a profound necessity.

To recreate oneself is to embark on a transformative journey of self-discovery, self-improvement, and self-reinvention. It is an intentional act of shedding old identities, beliefs, and limitations to embrace a new, empowered version of ourselves. This process requires courage, self-reflection, and a deep commitment to personal growth.

In this exploration of recreating oneself, we will delve into the transformative power it holds and the steps one can take to embark on this path of self-renewal. Through the stories of remarkable individuals who have successfully recreated themselves, we will witness the profound impact it can have on our lives and the world around us.

Embracing Change: The Catalyst for Transformation

Change is the catalyst that sparks the need for self-recreation. We will explore the various triggers and catalysts that can ignite the desire for personal transformation, whether it be a major life event, a realization of unfulfilled potential, or a longing for greater purpose and meaning.

Self-Reflection: The Key to Discovering Authenticity

To recreate oneself authentically, we must embark on a journey of self-reflection. By delving deep into our core values, passions, strengths, and weaknesses, we gain a clearer understanding of who we truly are. Through introspection, we can identify the aspects of ourselves that no longer serve us and those that we wish to nurture and cultivate.

Setting a Vision: Designing the Blueprint for Transformation

Creating a clear vision of the person we aspire to become is crucial in the process of recreating oneself. We will explore the power of setting meaningful goals, visualizing our desired future, and creating a roadmap for personal growth. By aligning our actions with our vision, we can move purposefully towards our new identity.

Breaking Free from Limiting Beliefs: Unleashing Inner Potential

Limiting beliefs are the shackles that hold us back from reaching our full potential. We will delve into the process of identifying and challenging these self-imposed limitations. Through adopting a growth mindset, cultivating self-compassion, and embracing resilience, we can break free from the constraints of our own minds and unlock our true capabilities.

Cultivating New Habits: Nurturing Positive Change

Recreating oneself requires the cultivation of new habits and behaviors that align with our desired identity. We will explore the power of habit formation, the role of discipline and consistency, and the importance of self-care in sustaining personal transformation. By consciously integrating new habits into our daily lives, we solidify the foundation for lasting change.

Embracing Uncertainty: Navigating the Challenges of Transformation

The journey of recreating oneself is not without challenges. We will examine the fears, doubts, and obstacles that can arise along the way. Through resilience, adaptability, and embracing uncertainty, we can navigate these challenges and use them as opportunities for growth and self-discovery.

Embodying the New Identity: Living Your Truth

True transformation occurs when we embody our new identity fully. We will explore the importance of self-expression, embracing authenticity, and stepping into our power with confidence. By aligning our thoughts, words, and actions with our recreated self, we can inspire others and create a positive ripple effect in the world.

Recreating oneself is a profound and empowering journey of personal growth and transformation. It is an invitation to shed old layers, and embrace change.

Illustration One

Once upon a time, in a quaint village nestled among rolling hills, there lived a young woman named Lily. Lily was a kind and compassionate soul, but she felt a growing sense of dissatisfaction and restlessness within her. She longed for something more, a deeper sense of purpose and fulfillment.

One day, as she wandered through the village market, Lily stumbled upon an old bookstore tucked away in a corner. Curiosity ignited within her, and she stepped inside, the scent of aged books filling her senses. As she perused the shelves, her eyes fell upon a weathered volume titled "The Art of Recreating Yourself."

Intrigued, Lily pulled the book from the shelf and settled into a cozy corner of the store. The pages whispered stories of individuals who had embarked on transformative journeys, reshaping their lives and finding newfound joy and purpose. The tales ignited a spark within Lily's heart, and she knew that this book held the key to her own metamorphosis.

Over the following weeks, Lily delved into the book's wisdom, immersing herself in stories of individuals who had recreated themselves against all odds. One particular story captured her attention—the tale of Amelia, a young woman who had transformed from a shy, reserved introvert into a confident and inspiring public speaker.

Intrigued by Amelia's journey, Lily sought her out, hoping to glean wisdom from her own experience. They met in a quaint café, their conversation filled with warmth and shared vulnerability. Amelia recounted her struggles, the fears that had held her back, and the transformative steps she had taken to recreate herself.

Inspired by Amelia's story, Lily realized that recreating herself required a deep inner journey. She began by examining her own fears and insecurities, acknowledging the beliefs that held her back from fully embracing her potential. With each realization, she felt a weight lift from her shoulders, creating space for growth and self-discovery.

Lily set about defining her vision, envisioning the person she aspired to become. She imagined a version of herself filled with confidence, compassion, and a burning desire to make a difference in the lives of others. With this vision firmly in mind, she charted a roadmap, outlining the steps she needed to take to bring her desired identity to life.

She confronted her self-doubt head-on, challenging the limiting beliefs that whispered in her ear. Lily surrounded herself with a supportive community, seeking guidance and encouragement from those who believed in her potential. With each small victory, her confidence grew, fueling her determination to continue on her path of self-recreation.

As Lily cultivated new habits aligned with her vision, she noticed a gradual transformation taking place. She started speaking up in social gatherings, sharing her ideas and insights with newfound courage. She sought opportunities to step outside her comfort zone, embracing uncertainty and embracing the unknown with a sense of curiosity and excitement.

Over time, Lily's metamorphosis became evident to those around her. Friends and family marveled at her newfound confidence and radiance. But more importantly, Lily felt a profound sense of inner fulfillment. She had tapped into her authentic self, embracing her unique gifts and using them to make a positive impact in the lives of others.

Through her journey of self-recreation, Lily realized that the process was not about becoming someone entirely new, but rather about uncovering the essence of who she truly was. She had shed the layers that no longer served her, allowing her authentic self to shine through.

Lily's story spread throughout the village, inspiring others to embark on their own journeys of self-recreation. The bookstore that had ignited her own transformation became a hub of shared stories and wisdom, a place where individuals gathered to support and encourage one another on their transformative paths.

And so, the village flourished with a community of individuals embracing the power of self-recreation. As Lily's story and the stories of others echoed through the streets, a ripple effect of personal transformation took hold. Now, dear reader, it is your turn to heed the call of self-recreation.

Within the pages of "The Art of Recreating Yourself," you will find inspiration, guidance, and the stories of those who have paved the way before you. Let their journeys ignite the spark within your own heart, propelling you towards a life of greater purpose, fulfillment, and authenticity.

Take a moment to reflect on your own life. Are there aspects that no longer resonate with who you truly are? Are there dreams and desires that have been pushed aside, waiting to be rediscovered? Embrace the power within you to recreate yourself, to shed the layers that no longer serve you, and to step into the fullness of your potential.

Begin by embracing change, for it is the catalyst that propels us forward. Embrace self-reflection and dive deep into the depths of your being, unearthing your values, passions, and aspirations. Set a vision for the person you aspire to become, and let it guide your every step.

Challenge the limiting beliefs that have held you back, for they are mere illusions that cloud your true potential. Cultivate new habits that align with your vision, and embrace the uncertainty that accompanies growth. With each small step, you will gain momentum and move closer to your recreated self.

Surround yourself with a supportive community, seeking the wisdom and encouragement of those who believe in your journey. Share your story, for it has the power to inspire others and ignite their own transformations. Remember that recreating yourself is not a solitary endeavor; it is a collective movement of individuals embracing their true essence.

As you recreate yourself, be patient and kind to yourself. Transformation takes time and effort. Embrace the setbacks and challenges as opportunities for growth and learning. Trust in your innate resilience and know that the journey itself is as valuable as the destination.

Now, open the book, step onto the path of self-recreation, and let your story intertwine with the stories of countless others who have embarked on this transformative journey. Embrace the power within you to recreate yourself and to live a life of authenticity, purpose, and joy.

The world awaits your unique gifts and contributions. Embrace the call to recreate yourself and become the fullest expression of who you truly are. As you do so, may your transformation not only uplift your own life but also inspire and empower those around you.

The time is now. The power is within you. Embrace the journey of self-recreation and unlock the limitless possibilities that await.

Secrete

KNOW YOUR FOLLOWERS

In the realm of leadership, there is a profound truth that lies at the core of success: knowing your followers. Like a skilled conductor who understands the unique talents and aspirations of each musician in the orchestra, an effective leader comprehends the intricacies and nuances of their team members. It is through this intimate knowledge that a leader can orchestrate harmony, unleash creativity, and ignite the collective brilliance of their followers. For within the depths of knowing your followers lies the key to unlocking their potential, fostering engagement, and propelling the team towards unprecedented heights.

Knowing your followers is the foundation upon which extraordinary achievements are built. Imagine a skilled navigator who embarks on a grand voyage. To steer the ship through treacherous waters and towards uncharted horizons, the captain must intimately understand the strengths, weaknesses, and aspirations of each member of the crew. In much the same way, an effective leader embarks on a profound exploration of their team, delving into the depths of their followers' unique identities, aspirations, and motivations.

Truly knowing your followers transcends surface-level acquaintance. It is a journey that requires time, effort, and genuine curiosity. It involves listening intently to their stories, understanding their perspectives, and recognizing the diverse tapestry of experiences that shape their lives. It is through this empathetic understanding that leaders can establish deep connections, nurture trust, and create an environment where individuals feel seen, valued, and empowered.

When a leader knows their followers on a profound level, they become catalysts for growth and transformation. They unearth hidden talents, awaken dormant passions, and provide the necessary support and guidance to nurture the full potential of each team member. By recognizing the unique strengths of individuals and aligning them with tasks that amplify their abilities, leaders create an orchestra where each instrument plays in perfect harmony, creating a symphony of excellence.

Moreover, knowing your followers enables a leader to tailor their leadership style to meet the individual needs of each team member. They understand that motivation is not a one-size-fits-all concept and that different individuals thrive under different conditions. With this knowledge in hand, leaders can inspire, guide, and challenge their followers in ways that resonate with their intrinsic motivations, unlocking their drive, and propelling them towards personal and collective success.

Furthermore, when leaders possess an intimate understanding of their followers, they can effectively anticipate challenges and provide the necessary support to overcome them. By recognizing the unique struggles and aspirations of each team member, leaders can offer guidance, encouragement, and resources that enable individuals to navigate obstacles with resilience and determination. In doing so, leaders become beacons of strength, guiding their followers through the stormy seas of adversity towards brighter horizons.

Ultimately, knowing your followers is a transformative journey that transcends the realms of leadership. It is an act of deep connection, profound empathy, and genuine care for the well-being and growth of others. It is through this intimate understanding that leaders can harness the collective power of their team, unlocking untapped potential, fostering collaboration, and creating an environment where innovation and excellence thrive.

So, let us embark on this captivating odyssey of knowing our followers. Listen with open hearts, learn with insatiable curiosity, and nurture relationships that transcend the bounds of hierarchy. By truly knowing our followers, we can unleash the full spectrum of their capabilities, kindle their passions, and forge a shared journey towards remarkable achievements. For within the tapestry of knowing lies the seeds of inspiration, unity, and extraordinary leadership.

In addition to the profound understanding and connection it fosters, knowing your followers brings forth a plethora of benefits that can elevate both the leader and the team to new heights. Let us explore some of these remarkable advantages:

Enhanced Communication

Knowing your followers allows for more effective and meaningful communication. By understanding their communication styles, preferences, and even non-verbal cues, leaders can tailor their messages to resonate with each individual. This leads to clearer understanding, improved collaboration, and stronger relationships within the team.

Increased Engagement and Motivation

When leaders possess deep knowledge of their followers, they can tap into their unique motivations and align them with meaningful work. By assigning tasks that leverage their strengths and passions, leaders foster a sense of purpose and fulfillment, resulting in increased engagement and motivation. As a result, team members become more committed, productive, and willing to go the extra mile.

Tailored Support and Development

Knowing your followers enables leaders to provide personalized support and development opportunities. By recognizing their strengths and areas for growth, leaders can offer targeted guidance, mentorship, and training that caters to the specific needs of each individual. This customized approach fosters personal and professional growth, empowering team members to reach their full potential.

Strengthened Trust and Collaboration

When leaders invest time and effort in getting to know their followers, trust flourishes. By demonstrating genuine care, empathy, and understanding, leaders create a safe and inclusive environment where individuals feel comfortable expressing themselves and sharing ideas. This cultivates a culture of collaboration, innovation, and psychological safety, enabling the team to tackle complex challenges together.

Improved Conflict Resolution

Knowing your followers equips leaders with insights into their unique perspectives, values, and backgrounds. This understanding enables leaders to address conflicts with empathy and fairness, finding resolutions that respect the diverse needs and interests of team members. By fostering open dialogue and creating a supportive environment, leaders can transform conflicts into opportunities for growth and strengthened relationships.

Higher Retention and Loyalty

When leaders truly know their followers, they create a sense of belonging and value. Team members feel seen, heard, and appreciated, leading to higher levels of job satisfaction and loyalty. This, in turn, increases retention rates and reduces turnover, allowing the team to maintain continuity and stability, while attracting top talent who are drawn to the positive and supportive culture.

Agility and Adaptability

Knowing your followers enables leaders to harness the collective strengths and perspectives of the team. This diversity of thought and experience fosters adaptability and agility, as leaders can draw upon the unique skills and insights of each individual to navigate change and seize opportunities. The team becomes more resilient and capable of embracing new challenges with confidence.

Empowered Leadership Succession

When leaders invest in knowing their followers, they foster a culture of leadership development and succession. By identifying emerging talents, nurturing their growth, and providing mentorship, leaders can groom future leaders within the organization. This creates a pipeline of capable and empowered individuals who can continue to drive the team and the organization forward.

The benefits of knowing your followers are abundant and far-reaching. From improved communication and engagement to stronger trust and collaboration, leaders who invest in understanding their team members create an environment that fosters growth, innovation, and high performance. By recognizing the individual strengths, motivations, and aspirations of each follower, leaders can unleash their full potential and lead their teams towards extraordinary achievements.

Recognize the immense value of truly knowing our followers. Commit to building meaningful connections, listening intently, and understanding the unique tapestry of experiences that shape their lives. By doing so, we can enhance communication, foster engagement and motivation, tailor support and development, strengthen trust and collaboration, resolve conflicts with empathy, and empower our teams to navigate change and embrace new opportunities.

Embark on this remarkable journey of knowing. Lead with intention, empathy, and a genuine desire to understand those who follow us. By embracing the power of knowing, we can unlock the full potential of our teams, foster an environment of growth and innovation, and create a legacy of exceptional leadership.

The call to action is clear: take the first step on this transformative path. Make time to connect with your team members on a deeper level. Listen actively, seek to understand their perspectives, and appreciate the unique qualities they bring to the table. Nurture an environment of trust, collaboration, and inclusivity. By knowing your followers, you will unlock the key to unlocking their potential and achieving remarkable results together.

Remember, leadership is not just about guiding from the front; it is about knowing and empowering those who stand beside us. So, let us embark on this journey of knowing, and together, we can create a future where leadership is driven by profound understanding, genuine connection, and collective success.

Secret

◆ 3 ◆

INDISPENSABILITY

In the vast embroidery of humanity, woven with countless lives and stories, there are selected group of individuals who transcend the ordinary and become truly indispensable. They are the rare gems that sparkle amidst the crowd, leaving an everlasting imprint on the lives they touch. Like the master craftsmen who intricately weave the threads of purpose and passion, these indispensable individuals weave themselves into the very fabric of our existence, enriching it with their unique blend of qualities and contributions.

An indispensable person is a beacon of light in a world that sometimes feels engulfed in darkness. They possess an innate ability to radiate positivity, hope, and unwavering belief in the human potential. Their presence has a transformative effect, uplifting spirits, igniting inspiration, and awakening dormant dreams. When they enter a room, the atmosphere becomes charged with an undeniable energy that inspires others to aim higher, reach further, and believe in the extraordinary.

These remarkable individuals are often characterized by their unwavering integrity, authenticity, and moral compass. They lead by example, upholding ethical principles and demonstrating an unwavering commitment to honesty, fairness, and compassion. Their words and actions are in perfect alignment, creating a sense of trust and reliability that draws people towards them like a magnet.

Moreover, indispensable individuals possess an innate ability to connect deeply with others. They have a profound understanding of the human condition and the power of empathy. They listen intently, not only to words but also to the unspoken, the nuances, and the emotions that lie beneath. With their compassionate hearts and open minds, they create a safe space for others to express themselves, share their vulnerabilities, and find solace in their presence.

In addition to their empathetic nature, indispensable individuals possess a remarkable gift for bringing out the best in those around them. They see potential where others see limitations and believe in others' abilities even when they doubt themselves. Their unwavering support and encouragement act as a catalyst for personal and professional growth, unlocking hidden talents, and inspiring others to push beyond their perceived boundaries.

Moreover, indispensable individuals are natural problem solvers and catalysts for change. They possess a unique blend of creativity, critical thinking, and resilience that enables them to navigate challenges with grace and determination. They see obstacles as opportunities for growth, learning, and innovation. Their presence in any endeavor infuses it with a sense of purpose, direction, and the unwavering belief that success is not only possible but inevitable.

An indispensable leader is a rare gem that enriches the world with their unique qualities, unwavering presence, and transformative impact. They uplift, inspire, and empower those around them, leaving an indelible mark on hearts and minds. In a world that often craves authenticity, compassion, and leadership, these remarkable individuals embody the very essence of what it means to be indispensable. Their contributions shape the course of history, and their legacy resonates long after they have left our lives. So let us celebrate and honor the indispensable individuals among us, for they are the guiding lights that illuminate our path towards a brighter, more compassionate, and fulfilling world.

In addition to their extraordinary qualities and transformative impact, indispensable individuals bring forth a myriad of benefits that ripple through personal and professional realms. Let us delve into some of these remarkable advantages:

Inspiration and Motivation

The presence of an indispensable person is a wellspring of inspiration and motivation. Their unwavering belief in the potential of others ignites a fire within, encouraging individuals to pursue their dreams, overcome obstacles, and strive for excellence. Their contagious enthusiasm and passion create an atmosphere where creativity flourishes, pushing people to think beyond limits and tap into their fullest potential.

Growth and Development

Indispensable individuals are catalysts for personal and professional growth. They provide invaluable guidance, support, and mentorship, helping others recognize their strengths, identify areas for improvement, and unlock their hidden potential. Through their wisdom, experience, and constructive feedback, they propel individuals towards continuous learning, self-reflection, and growth.

Collaboration and Teamwork

The presence of an indispensable person fosters a culture of collaboration and teamwork. Their ability to connect with others on a deep level and create a sense of trust and psychological safety encourages open communication, collaboration, and the exchange of diverse ideas. They bridge gaps, dissolve conflicts, and bring together individuals with different perspectives, skills, and backgrounds, fostering a harmonious and high-performing team.

Resilience and Adaptability

Indispensable individuals possess a remarkable resilience and adaptability that influences those around them. They navigate challenges and setbacks with grace, inspiring others to persevere and embrace change. Their positive outlook, problem-solving skills, and ability to see opportunities in adversity instill a sense of resilience and optimism within the team, enabling them to thrive in dynamic and unpredictable environments.

Enhanced Relationships and Trust

The presence of an indispensable person nurtures deeper connections and fosters trust within relationships. Their empathetic nature, active listening, and genuine interest in others create an environment where individuals feel seen, heard, and valued. This cultivates strong bonds, promotes effective communication, and builds a foundation of trust that allows for greater collaboration, synergy, and mutual support.

Positive Organizational Culture

Indispensable individuals contribute to the development of a positive organizational culture. Their authentic leadership style, ethical values, and commitment to fairness and inclusivity set the tone for a healthy and thriving work environment. They inspire a shared vision, promote a sense of purpose, and cultivate a culture of respect, integrity, and continuous improvement.

Organizational Success

The presence of indispensable individuals has a direct impact on organizational success. Their ability to inspire and motivate others, foster collaboration and innovation, and navigate challenges with resilience contributes to achieving strategic goals, driving performance, and delivering exceptional results. Their vision, guidance, and unwavering commitment set the stage for organizational success and create a legacy that transcends their time.

The benefits of an indispensable individual extend far and wide, impacting individuals, teams, and organizations as a whole. They inspire, guide, and empower others, fostering growth, collaboration, and resilience. Through their exceptional qualities, they shape organizational culture, drive success, and leave an enduring legacy. So let us recognize and cherish the indispensable individuals among us, for their contributions and influence are immeasurable, and their impact is a testament to the transformative power of their presence.

In a world longing for exceptional leaders and transformative change, the time has come to answer the call and rise as indispensable individuals. We are called to be the catalysts of inspiration, the champions of progress, and the architects of a better tomorrow. The stakes are high, and the need is urgent.

Imagine a world where ordinary becomes extraordinary, where mediocrity is replaced by greatness, and where every individual is empowered to unleash their full potential. It starts with you. It starts with your commitment to becoming an indispensable force in the lives of those around you.

Now is the time to dig deep within yourself and unearth the unique qualities that set you apart. Embrace your authenticity, your passions, and your purpose. Let them guide your actions, inspire your decisions, and fuel your relentless pursuit of excellence. The world craves authenticity, and it is through your genuine presence that you can ignite the flames of inspiration in others.

Empathy is your superpower. Listen intently, not just with your ears, but with your heart. Seek to understand the struggles, dreams, and aspirations of those you encounter. Your ability to connect on a deep level, to empathize with their journey, and to uplift their spirits will set you apart as an indispensable leader.

Continuous growth is your mantra. Commit to lifelong learning, for knowledge is the foundation upon which greatness is built. Seek out new experiences, expand your horizons, and push the boundaries of your comfort zone. Embrace failure as a stepping stone to success, and let resilience be your guiding light in times of adversity.

Collaboration is your secret weapon. Recognize that no one achieves greatness alone. Cultivate an environment of trust, respect, and collaboration, where ideas are freely shared and diverse perspectives are celebrated. Create a space where every voice is heard, every contribution is valued, and where the collective genius of the team is unleashed.

Integrity is your compass. Let your actions align with your values, and let your integrity be the bedrock upon which trust is built. Lead by example, displaying unwavering ethics, honesty, and transparency. Your integrity will inspire others to follow your lead and to strive for greatness with unwavering commitment.

The world needs you, now more than ever. Your unique blend of qualities, your unwavering determination, and your relentless pursuit of excellence have the power to shape the future. It is through your indispensable presence that transformation occurs, organizations thrive, and lives are forever changed.

So, let us stand together, united in our pursuit of greatness. Let us embrace the challenges that lie ahead and emerge stronger, more resilient, and more indispensable than ever before. The time has come for us to unleash our full potential, to inspire those around us, and to leave an indelible mark on the world.

Be the indispensable leader that this world needs. Embrace the call to greatness, ignite the flames of inspiration, and be the change that the world yearns for. The future awaits, and it is in your hands to shape it. Let us embark on this extraordinary journey together, knowing that our collective impact will resonate far beyond our wildest dreams.

Secrete

UNIQUENESS

In a world saturated with information and endless options, the need to be unique and stand out has never been more crucial. Whether in personal relationships, professional pursuits, or creative endeavors, embracing and showcasing our individuality sets us apart from the crowd.

Leadership is not simply about holding a position of authority; it is about inspiring and influencing others to achieve greatness. In today's dynamic and competitive world, the need for unique leaders has never been more crucial. This chapter of the book explores the journey to becoming a unique leader, delving into the key qualities, strategies, and mindset necessary to unleash your authentic leadership potential. By embracing your individuality and cultivating your unique strengths, you can make a profound impact, inspire others, and create a legacy that stands the test of time.

THE LEADERSHIP MANUAL

1. Distinguishing Yourself from the Noise.

In a society where conformity often reigns, being unique allows you to break free from the sea of sameness. By embracing your distinct qualities, talents, and perspectives, you create a space where your voice can be heard above the noise. Standing out enables you to capture attention, spark curiosity, and leave a lasting impression on others.

2. Attracting Opportunities and Success

When you present yourself as unique, you become a magnet for opportunities. Employers, collaborators, and clients are drawn to individuals who possess a one-of-a-kind blend of skills, ideas, and experiences. By standing out, you position yourself as an asset, increasing your chances of professional advancement, career opportunities, and entrepreneurial success.

3. Authenticity and Connection

Authenticity is a powerful force that fosters genuine connections with others. By embracing your uniqueness, you attract like-minded individuals who appreciate and resonate with your true self. When you stand out, you create a tribe of supporters, collaborators, and friends who value you for who you are, enhancing personal relationships and creating a sense of belonging.

4. Inspiring Innovation and Creativity

Uniqueness breeds innovation and fuels creativity. By embracing your individuality, you bring fresh perspectives, unconventional ideas, and novel solutions to the table. When you stand out, you inspire others to think outside the box, challenge the status quo, and push the boundaries of what is possible. Your uniqueness becomes a catalyst for progress and transformation.

5. Leaving a Lasting Legacy

We all have a deep desire to leave a mark on the world. By embracing your uniqueness and standing out, you create a legacy that is uniquely yours. Your distinct contributions, ideas, and achievements become a part of the collective human tapestry, shaping the future and inspiring generations to come.

...Take Away

Becoming a unique leader is a journey of self-discovery, continuous growth, and intentional development. By cultivating self-awareness, embracing authenticity, and honing your leadership skills, you can unleash your authentic leadership potential. Through visionary leadership, effective communication, and leading with integrity, you can inspire others, foster innovation, and leave a lasting legacy. Embrace your uniqueness, lead with purpose, and make a profound impact as a truly remarkable and distinctive leader.

Illustration Two

Once upon a time in the bustling kingdom of Veridia, there was a young woman named Amelia. Amelia possessed an innate desire to make a difference and lead with purpose. However, she realized that she needed to embark on a transformative journey to become a unique leader.

Amelia set out on her quest, guided by an ancient map handed down through generations. The first stop on her journey was the Cave of Self-Awareness. Deep within its depths, she encountered a wise old sage who challenged her to look within herself. Through introspection, Amelia discovered her values, passions, and purpose. She understood that her uniqueness lay in embracing her true self and aligning her leadership style with her authentic identity.

Next, Amelia found herself in the Enchanted Forest of Vision. As she wandered through the towering trees, she stumbled upon a mystical fountain. Gazing into its shimmering waters, Amelia saw visions of a better future. She realized the importance of crafting a compelling vision that would inspire and motivate others. With clarity and determination, she developed a vision that would guide her and her team towards success.

Continuing her journey, Amelia reached the Valley of Communication. Here, she encountered a group of diverse individuals with unique stories and perspectives. She learned the art of active listening and discovered the power of effective communication. Amelia understood that her words held the ability to inspire, motivate, and bring people together. Through storytelling and empathetic connection, she influenced and inspired those around her.

As Amelia ventured further, she encountered the Storm of Challenges. Strong winds and heavy rain battered her, threatening to deter her progress. But Amelia's resilience shone through as she weathered the storm with unwavering determination. She understood that setbacks and obstacles were opportunities for growth and learning. Her ability to navigate through challenges demonstrated her strength as a leader.

In the final leg of her journey, Amelia arrived at the Palace of Integrity. The palace was guarded by the virtue of ethics and honesty. Amelia understood the importance of leading with integrity, making ethical decisions, and holding herself accountable. She fostered a culture of trust and fairness, building strong relationships based on respect and transparency.

As Amelia returned to Veridia, her transformation was evident to all who knew her. Her authenticity radiated from within, capturing the hearts and minds of those she led. Her unique leadership style inspired innovation, collaboration, and personal growth among her team members. The kingdom thrived under her guidance, and her influence extended far beyond its borders.

Amelia's journey taught her that being a unique leader was not about imitating others or conforming to societal expectations. It was about embracing her individuality, leading with purpose, and making a lasting impact. Her tale became a legend, passed down through generations, inspiring future leaders to embark on their own quests to unleash their authentic leadership potential.

And so, the kingdom of Veridia flourished under the reign of a truly remarkable and unique leader—Amelia, who proved that embracing one's uniqueness was the key to unlocking greatness and leaving a lasting legacy.

And as the tale of Amelia, the unique leader, comes to an end, let her journey serve as a call to action for all aspiring leaders who seek to make a difference. It is time for you to embark on your own quest to unleash your authentic leadership potential.

Reflect on your values, passions, and purpose. Embrace your true self and align your leadership style with your authentic identity. Craft a compelling vision that inspires and motivates others. Develop effective communication skills to connect deeply with those around you. Embrace challenges as opportunities for growth and resilience. Lead with integrity, making ethical decisions and fostering a culture of trust.

Now is the time to step forward, to embrace your uniqueness, and to make your mark as a leader. The world is waiting for your distinct voice, your innovative ideas, and your unwavering dedication to creating a positive impact.

Remember, your journey may not be easy. It may require courage, perseverance, and continuous learning. But as you embrace your authenticity, you will inspire those around you, cultivate meaningful relationships, and leave a lasting legacy.

So, heed the call to action, unleash your authentic leadership potential, and let your unique brilliance shine forth. The time is now. The world is ready for your extraordinary leadership.

Secrete

BE ATTRACTIVE

In the realm of leadership, there are those exceptional individuals who possess an undeniable allure—an irresistible charisma that draws others towards them. They effortlessly inspire and motivate, leaving a lasting impact on the hearts and minds of those they lead.

In the vast landscape of leadership, where countless individuals strive to make an impact, there exists a rare breed of leaders who possess an undeniable allure—an essence that transcends the ordinary and captivates the hearts and minds of those around them. These attractive leaders possess a magnetic presence, an irresistible charm, and an innate ability to inspire, motivate, and rally others towards a shared vision. But what exactly sets them apart? Is it a combination of charisma, confidence, and effective communication? Or is it something deeper, rooted in their authenticity and emotional intelligence?

WHY YOU MUST BE ATTRACTIVE

Enhanced Engagement and Satisfaction

An attractive leader has the ability to engage and connect with their team members on a deep level. By demonstrating genuine care, empathy, and support, they create an environment where their followers feel valued, heard, and motivated. This, in turn, leads to higher levels of engagement and satisfaction among team members. When employees are engaged, they are more likely to be productive, committed, and willing to go the extra mile to achieve the team's goals.

Improved Team Collaboration and Synergy

An attractive leader understands the importance of collaboration and fosters an environment that promotes teamwork and synergy. They encourage open communication, value diverse perspectives, and create a safe space for individuals to contribute their ideas. By building strong relationships and fostering a sense of camaraderie, attractive leaders facilitate effective collaboration among team members. This collaboration leads to increased creativity, innovation, and problem-solving capabilities within the team.

Increased Loyalty and Retention

An attractive leader not only inspires their team members but also earns their loyalty. When followers feel valued, supported, and motivated by their leader, they develop a strong sense of loyalty towards the team. This loyalty translates into increased employee retention, reducing turnover and the associated costs. Team members are more likely to stay with their team that has an attractive leader who genuinely cares about their well-being and development.

Positive Organizational Culture

The presence of an attractive leader has a profound impact on organizational culture. They set the tone by embodying the values, vision, and purpose of the team. Through their charisma, authenticity, and ability to connect with others, they inspire and influence their team members to embrace those values and contribute to a positive culture. An attractive leader fosters an environment of trust, respect, and collaboration, creating a culture where employees thrive, feel empowered, and are motivated to give their best.

Increased Performance and Business Success

The influence of an attractive leader extends beyond individual and team levels—it impacts the overall performance and success of the organization. When members of the team are engaged, satisfied, and motivated, their performance improves. They are more productive, innovative, and focused on achieving organizational goals. With an attractive leader at the helm, organizations experience increased efficiency, effectiveness, and a competitive edge in the market. The ability of attractive leaders to inspire and drive their teams towards success directly contributes to the overall success of the organization.

The importance of an attractive leader cannot be overstated. From inspiring and motivating team members to fostering collaboration, loyalty, and a positive organizational culture, attractive leaders create an environment that drives success. Their ability to engage, connect, and influence others unlocks the full potential of individuals and teams, resulting in enhanced performance, employee satisfaction, and overall business success. Organizations that recognize the value of an attractive leader and invest in developing attractive leadership capabilities are poised to thrive in an increasingly competitive landscape.

BECOMING AN ATTRACTIVE LEADER

Lets embark on a brief journey to unravel the secrets of the attractive leader—those remarkable individuals who effortlessly draw others towards them. Let's delve into the multifaceted qualities and strategies that contribute to their appeal, exploring the intricacies of their charismatic presence, their masterful communication skills, and their unparalleled ability to forge meaningful connections. Through the lens of their remarkable journeys, we uncover some key traits and practices that make them irresistible forces of leadership.

SOME KEY STEPS TO CONSIDER

Self-Awareness

In the realm of leadership, self-awareness is the key that unlocks the doors to personal growth, authentic connection, and effective decision-making. It is the foundation upon which great leaders are built—the power to understand oneself, harness strengths, and navigate weaknesses with clarity and purpose. Self-awareness is not just a buzzword; it is a transformative tool that allows leaders to truly know themselves, their values, and their impact on others.

Self-awareness is the cornerstone of personal and professional growth. It is the ability to introspect and gain deep insights into one's thoughts, emotions, strengths, weaknesses, and values. In the context of leadership, self-awareness is paramount. It empowers leaders to understand their impact on others, make informed decisions, and cultivate authenticity.

Authenticity

Authenticity is a magnetic force that draws people in, inspires trust, and fuels genuine connections. In a world often filled with façades and pretenses, embracing authenticity is a revolutionary act. It is about being true to yourself, expressing your values and beliefs, and leading from a place of genuine sincerity.

WHY YOU MUST BE AUTHENTIC

Trust and Credibility: Authentic leaders build trust by aligning their actions with their values, creating credibility among team members.

Engagement: Authentic leaders foster an environment where team members feel safe to express their ideas, leading to higher engagement and satisfaction.

Inspiration and Role Modeling: Authentic leaders inspire and motivate others to embrace their true selves, bringing unique perspectives and talents.

Effective Decision-Making: Authentic leaders make principled decisions that align with their values, fostering trust and clarity among team members.

Effective Communication Skills

Effective communication is the lifeblood of attractive leadership. It is the art of connecting with others, conveying ideas, and inspiring action.

They have a profound impact on building trust, enhancing collaboration, inspiring motivation, and resolving conflicts. To develop effective communication skills, you should practice active listening, strive for clarity and conciseness, utilize non-verbal communication effectively, cultivate empathy and emotional intelligence, adapt their communication style, encourage feedback and collaboration, leverage the power of storytelling, establish clarity in expectations, master conflict resolution, and embrace continuous improvement. By honing these skills, leaders can build bridges, inspire change, and create a positive impact on their teams and organizations. Effective communication is a powerful tool that enables leaders to connect, engage, and inspire others.

Remember, effective communication is not just about what you say, but also how you say it, how you listen, and how you connect with others. Unlock the power of effective communication skills, and watch as you transform into a leader who inspires, motivates, and makes a lasting impact.

Compelling Vision

A compelling vision is a crucial asset for anyone that desires to attract followers and compel them to stays, as it has a profound impact on individuals and teams. It inspires and motivates, aligns efforts, engages and empowers team members, and stimulates innovation and growth. To craft and communicate a compelling vision, leaders should focus on painting a clear and inspiring picture, aligning it with core values and mission, making it ambitious and stretching, involving and engaging their team, communicating with passion and clarity, creating a roadmap with milestones, fostering collaboration, and leading by example. Embracing the power of a compelling vision allows leaders to inspire change, achieve extraordinary results, and leave a lasting impact on their teams and organizations.

As a leader, your ability to craft and communicate a compelling vision is a catalyst for success. A compelling vision inspires and motivates, provides direction and focus, engages and empowers, and stimulates innovation and growth. Embrace the power of a compelling vision and use it as a guiding force on your leadership journey. By crafting a vision that captivates hearts and minds, you have the potential to inspire change, achieve extraordinary results, and leave a lasting legacy as a leader.

Remember, becoming an attractive leader is a journey that requires dedication, self-reflection, and a commitment to personal growth. By following these guidelines and adapting them to your own unique circumstances, you can unleash your potential as an attractive leader who inspires and motivates others towards greatness.

Illustration Three

Once upon a time, in a bustling city, there was a small startup company called InnovateTech. The company was on the brink of collapse, facing internal conflicts and dwindling morale among its employees. In desperate need of a turnaround, the board of directors decided to bring in a new leader who could inject new life into the organization.

Enter Sarah Mitchell, a remarkable leader with a magnetic presence and a reputation for transforming struggling companies into thriving enterprises. Sarah possessed an innate ability to attract and inspire others, and her success stories had become the stuff of legends. As she stepped into her new role as CEO of InnovateTech, the employees couldn't help but be curious and intrigued by this charismatic leader.

On her first day, Sarah gathered the entire team in the company's spacious conference room. Instead of launching into a grandiose speech, she surprised everyone by sharing a personal story about her humble beginnings and the challenges she had faced throughout her career. Her vulnerability and authenticity immediately connected with the employees, as they saw a leader who was not only competent but also relatable.

Over the next few weeks, Sarah immersed herself in the company culture, making a point to engage with each employee on a personal level. She would have casual conversations during lunch breaks, asking about their passions and goals. Through active listening and genuine empathy, Sarah created an environment where everyone felt heard, valued, and understood.

Sarah also understood the power of effective communication. During team meetings, she would captivate her audience with compelling stories and vivid metaphors that illustrated the company's vision and goals. Her words had a profound impact, igniting a sense of purpose and passion among the employees. Sarah's messages were tailored to resonate with different individuals and departments, ensuring that everyone felt included and motivated to contribute their best.

In addition to her charismatic presence and powerful communication, Sarah was a firm believer in collaboration and teamwork. She encouraged cross-functional projects, bringing together employees from various departments to work towards common objectives. By fostering a sense of camaraderie and synergy, Sarah created an environment where creativity flourished, and innovative ideas emerged.

But Sarah's attractiveness as a leader went beyond her engaging demeanor and collaborative spirit. She genuinely cared about the personal and professional growth of her team members. She initiated mentorship programs, pairing experienced employees with those seeking guidance. She invested in training and development opportunities, providing resources and support for individuals to enhance their skills and knowledge.

As time went on, InnovateTech began to thrive under Sarah's leadership. Employee morale soared, conflicts dissipated, and productivity reached new heights. The company became known not only for its innovative products but also for its extraordinary workplace culture, attracting top talents from the industry.

Sarah's journey to becoming an attractive leader was not without its challenges. She had to overcome obstacles, navigate difficult decisions, and continuously reflect on her own leadership style. But through her unwavering commitment to self-awareness, continuous learning, and genuine connection with her team, she was able to unleash her charismatic potential and inspire others to reach their full potential.

The path to becoming an attractive leader is not about acquiring a superficial charm or following a set of rigid steps. It is about embracing authenticity, empathy, and effective communication. It is about fostering meaningful relationships and creating an environment where individuals feel valued and inspired. Like Sarah, you too can embark on this transformative journey, cultivating your own unique brand of leadership and becoming an attractive force that inspires greatness in others. So, go forth with courage, empathy, and a genuine desire to make a difference, and watch as your leadership becomes irresistible to those around you.

As we conclude this journey into the realm of becoming an attractive leader, it is essential to remember that leadership is not a destination but a continuous process of growth and development. The steps and strategies we have explored in this exposition provide a solid foundation for enhancing your leadership presence and inspiring others. However, true transformation can only occur through action.

Therefore, I encourage you to take the next step and put these insights into practice. Begin by cultivating self-awareness and reflecting on your strengths, weaknesses, values, and purpose as a leader. Embrace authenticity and let your true self shine through in your interactions. Master the art of effective communication, both verbal and nonverbal, and learn to tailor your message to different audiences. Develop your active listening skills and foster empathy in your relationships. Build trust, encourage collaboration, and invest in the growth and development of your team members.

But above all, remember that becoming an attractive leader is not about seeking personal glory or exerting power over others. It is about creating a positive impact, inspiring others to reach their full potential, and fostering a culture of excellence and innovation.

So, take action today. Implement these steps, adapt them to your unique circumstances, and observe the ripple effect they have on your leadership journey. Embrace every challenge as an opportunity for growth, and be open to feedback and continuous improvement. By doing so, you will not only become an attractive leader but also contribute to a brighter future for your organization and the people you lead.

Now is the time to unleash your charisma, embrace authenticity, and inspire others with your leadership. The world is in need of attractive leaders who can ignite passion, drive change, and make a meaningful difference. Are you ready to step up and become that leader? The choice is yours. Embrace the challenge, embark on this transformative journey, and let your magnetic presence inspire greatness in others.

Secrete

RESILIENCE

Resilience is a fundamental quality that sets exceptional leaders apart. In the face of adversity, a resilient leader stands strong, maintains composure, and inspires others to persevere. They possess the unique ability to bounce back from setbacks, learn from failures, and adapt to ever-changing circumstances. A resilient leader not only withstands challenges but uses them as opportunities for growth and transformation.

One defining characteristic of a resilient leader is their unwavering determination. They refuse to let obstacles define their journey or deter them from their goals. Instead, they embrace challenges as stepping stones to success. When faced with setbacks, they exhibit a positive mindset, focusing on solutions rather than dwelling on problems.

They inspire their team members to adopt the same mindset, fostering a culture of resilience and optimism.

A resilient leader also understands the importance of self-care and well-being. They recognize that their own resilience is directly tied to their physical and mental health. They prioritize self-care practices such as exercise, meditation, and taking breaks to recharge. By modeling self-care, they show their team members the significance of maintaining balance and managing stress in high-pressure situations.

Furthermore, a resilient leader excels in communication and relationship-building. They foster an open and supportive environment where team members feel comfortable sharing their challenges and seeking guidance. They provide a listening ear, offer empathy, and provide constructive feedback. Through effective communication, they ensure that their team members feel supported, valued, and motivated to overcome obstacles.

Adaptability is another key quality of a resilient leader. They understand that change is inevitable, and they embrace it with flexibility and agility. They are quick to adjust strategies, pivot when necessary, and seek new opportunities amidst uncertainty. By demonstrating adaptability, they instill confidence in their team, fostering a spirit of innovation and resilience in the face of change.

A resilient leader possesses a unique set of qualities that enable them to navigate challenges with strength and determination. Their unwavering resolve, focus on solutions, commitment to self-care, effective communication, and adaptability set them apart as exceptional leaders. By embodying resilience, they inspire their teams to rise above adversity, fostering a culture of growth, innovation, and success. In a world filled with uncertainties, the resilient leader is a beacon of hope, guiding their team towards a brighter future.

Becoming a resilient leader is not just a personal endeavor; it holds immense importance in the realm of leadership and organizational success. Here are some key reasons why developing resilience is crucial for your leadership journey:

Navigating Uncertainty

In today's fast-paced and ever-changing world, uncertainty is inevitable. Resilient leaders possess the ability to navigate ambiguity and adapt to unforeseen circumstances. They remain calm and composed, providing stability and direction for their teams even in the face of uncertainty.

Inspiring and Motivating Others

Resilient leaders serve as beacons of hope and inspiration for their teams. By demonstrating resilience in their own actions and attitudes, they inspire others to persevere and maintain a positive outlook during challenging times. Their resilience becomes contagious, fostering a collective spirit of determination and resilience within the organization.

Overcoming Adversity

Adversity is an inherent part of any leadership journey. Resilient leaders possess the mental and emotional strength to face adversity head-on, learning from setbacks and using them as catalysts for growth. Their ability to bounce back from failure or setbacks not only builds their own character but also instills confidence in their team members.

Problem Solving and Decision Making

Resilient leaders are adept at problem-solving and making effective decisions under pressure. They remain level-headed and think critically, finding creative solutions to complex problems. Their resilience enables them to stay focused, identify opportunities within challenges, and make sound decisions that propel the organization forward.

Building Strong Relationships

Resilient leaders prioritize building strong and supportive relationships within their teams and across the organization. They actively listen, show empathy, and provide a safe space for open communication. By fostering a culture of support and trust, resilient leaders create an environment where individuals feel empowered to overcome challenges together.

Managing Change

Change is a constant in today's dynamic business landscape. Resilient leaders embrace change and guide their teams through transitions with confidence and adaptability. They communicate effectively, manage resistance, and help individuals navigate the emotional impact of change. Their resilience enables them to lead with a sense of purpose and direction during times of transformation.

Sustaining High Performance

Resilient leaders create an environment that supports high performance and productivity. They understand the importance of work-life balance, stress management, and self-care. By prioritizing the well-being of their team members, resilient leaders ensure sustainable success and prevent burnout.

Learning and Growth

Resilient leaders are lifelong learners, continuously seeking opportunities for personal and professional growth. They embrace feedback, learn from their experiences, and seek new knowledge and skills to enhance their leadership capabilities. Their resilience fuels a growth mindset, allowing them to adapt, evolve, and stay ahead in a rapidly changing world.

The importance of becoming a resilient leader cannot be overstated. Resilience equips leaders with the tools to navigate uncertainty, inspire others, overcome adversity, solve problems, build relationships, manage change, sustain high performance, and foster continuous learning and growth. By cultivating resilience within themselves and their teams, leaders create a foundation for success in the face of challenges and pave the way for a thriving and resilient organization

Illustration Four

In the heart of a bustling city, Sarah stood as a beacon of resilience and leadership. Her journey as the head of a tech startup was a rollercoaster ride of challenges and triumphs, but it was her unwavering determination and unbreakable spirit that set her apart.

One fateful day, disaster struck. A critical investor abruptly withdrew their support, sending shockwaves through the company. The air was heavy with uncertainty, and doubts began to creep into the minds of Sarah's team. But she refused to let despair take hold.

Gathering her team, Sarah opened up about her own personal struggles and failures. With a raw vulnerability, she shared the story of a time when her dreams shattered and her entrepreneurial venture crumbled. Her voice quivered with emotion as she recounted the sleepless nights and the tears shed, painting a vivid picture of the pain she endured.

Yet, Sarah's story did not end there. Through the haze of disappointment, she found the strength to rise again. The fire within her burned brighter than ever as she picked up the broken pieces and rebuilt her dreams from scratch. The scars etched on her soul became the foundation for her resilience.

Tears welled up in the eyes of her team members as they listened to her tale of courage and tenacity. In that moment, they saw a leader who had weathered the storms, faced adversity head-on, and emerged stronger. Inspired by Sarah's unwavering belief in their collective abilities, they found renewed hope and determination.

With passion and unwavering determination, Sarah rallied her team. She infused them with the belief that setbacks were not roadblocks but opportunities for growth and innovation. As they huddled together, brainstorming creative solutions, the energy in the room shifted from desolation to determination.

Sarah's leadership was not just about guiding her team; it was about lifting them up, nurturing their souls, and igniting the fire of resilience within each individual. She listened intently to their fears, offering a shoulder to lean on and a reassuring smile to wipe away their tears. Her empathy was a balm for their wounded spirits.

Days turned into weeks, and slowly but surely, the team's efforts began to bear fruit. New investors emerged, drawn by the unwavering spirit that radiated from Sarah and her team. The once uncertain future transformed into a beacon of hope, with each victory solidifying their resilience and resolve.

The tale of Sarah's leadership spread throughout the city, touching the hearts of aspiring leaders and emboldening them to face their own trials with unwavering determination. Her story became a testament to the power of resilience, a reminder that within each challenge lies the seed of opportunity.

In the end, Sarah's resilience not only saved the company but also created a legacy. Her leadership transformed a group of individuals into a tight-knit family bonded by shared experiences and an unbreakable spirit. Their success was not just measured in financial gains but in the unwavering strength they discovered within themselves.

Sarah's emotional journey of resilience continues to inspire others to embrace their own battles and emerge victorious. Her story serves as a powerful reminder that true leaders are not immune to struggles; rather, they are defined by their ability to rise above them, to transform pain into purpose, and to inspire others to do the same.

As the sun sets on the city, Sarah stands tall as a symbol of hope, her unwavering spirit illuminating the path for future generations. Through her emotional and compelling journey, she taught us that resilience is not just a quality; it is a way of life, a guiding force that enables leaders to overcome the darkest storms and leave a lasting impact on the world.

In the face of adversity and uncertainty, the story of Sarah, the resilient leader, serves as a powerful call to action. It urges us to embrace our own journeys with unwavering determination, to rise above challenges, and to become the leaders we aspire to be.

Let Sarah's story be a catalyst for change in our own lives. Let us dare to dream, to take risks, and to pursue our passions with unyielding courage. In the face of setbacks and failures, let us remember that resilience is not just a trait reserved for the chosen few; it is a skill that can be cultivated and strengthened.

As aspiring leaders, we must take the lessons of Sarah's resilience to heart. We must embody her unwavering belief in the power of human spirit and our ability to overcome any obstacle. Let us foster an environment of support and empathy, where our team members can find solace and strength in our leadership.

Furthermore, let us be the catalysts for resilience in our organizations and communities. By sharing our own stories of triumph over adversity, we inspire others to rise above their own challenges. Let us be the ones who ignite the flames of hope and determination in the hearts of those around us.

In our pursuit of becoming resilient leaders, let us prioritize self-care and well-being. By taking care of ourselves, we cultivate the strength needed to navigate the inevitable storms that lie ahead. Let us prioritize our physical, mental, and emotional health, knowing that our resilience is rooted in our ability to nurture ourselves.

Lastly, let us remember that resilience is not a destination but a lifelong journey. It requires continuous self-reflection, growth, and adaptation.

As we encounter new challenges and setbacks, let us embrace them as opportunities for growth and transformation. Let us forge ahead with unwavering determination, knowing that our resilience has the power to shape not only our own lives but also the lives of those we lead.

So, let Sarah's story be the spark that ignites the flame of resilience within us. Let us commit to becoming leaders who embody strength, courage, and unwavering determination. Together, we can create a world where resilience is celebrated, obstacles are transformed into opportunities, and the human spirit shines brightest in the face of adversity.

Take Home Note

In the world of leadership, mastery is not achieved in a single moment, but through a continuous journey of growth and learning. As we come to the end of this transformative journey, we can confidently say that Commanding Success is an ongoing pursuit that requires dedication, self-reflection, and a commitment to continuous growth. Throughout this book, we have explored the fundamental principles and strategies that underpin effective leadership, equipping you with the knowledge and insights to navigate the complex challenges of leadership with confidence and grace.

We have delved deep into the realms of mindset, exploring the power of a growth-oriented perspective that embraces change, embraces failure as a stepping stone to success, and continuously seeks opportunities for personal and professional development. We have examined the vital importance of self-awareness, understanding our strengths and weaknesses, and how they influence our leadership style and impact on those we lead.

Moreover, we have explored the essential skills and competencies that empower leaders to inspire, motivate, and empower their teams. We have learned the art of effective communication, mastering both verbal and non-verbal cues to foster connection and understanding. We have delved into the significance of emotional intelligence, cultivating empathy and creating an environment of trust and collaboration. We have discovered the power of strategic thinking and decision-making, and the ability to navigate ambiguity and complexity with clarity and purpose.

Now, armed with these invaluable tools and insights, it is time for you to step into your full leadership potential. Embrace the challenges that lie ahead as opportunities for growth and transformation. Cultivate a mindset of lifelong learning, seeking out new knowledge and experiences to broaden your horizons and expand your leadership repertoire. Surround yourself with a network of support, mentors, and peers who will challenge and inspire you to become the best leader you can be.

As you embark on your leadership journey, remember that your impact extends far beyond the confines of your immediate sphere of influence. Your ability to inspire and empower others has the potential to create a ripple effect, fostering a culture of excellence and positively shaping the lives of those you lead.

Now is the time to take action and embark on your path to Commanding Success. Reflect on the insights and strategies shared in this book, and identify the areas where you can grow and enhance your leadership capabilities. Develop a personalized action plan that incorporates specific goals, timelines, and milestones to keep you accountable.

Seek out opportunities for growth and learning, whether through attending leadership workshops and conferences, engaging in executive coaching, or pursuing advanced education in leadership studies. Embrace feedback as a valuable gift and actively seek input from your team, colleagues, and mentors to continuously refine and improve your leadership approach.

As you navigate your leadership journey, remember to stay true to your values and lead with integrity. Be authentic and transparent in your interactions, and cultivate a culture of trust, respect, and inclusivity within your team or organization. Celebrate the accomplishments of others and foster a supportive environment that encourages collaboration and innovation.

Together, let us rise as leaders who make a lasting impact. Let us embrace the art of powerful leadership and create a future where inspired and empowered individuals come together to drive meaningful change. The world needs leaders like you—leaders who are willing to step up, take charge, and make a difference.

Now, go forth and lead with purpose, passion, and unwavering determination. Your journey to Commanding Success starts now.

www.ingramcontent.com/pod-product-compliance
Lightning Source LLC
Chambersburg PA
CBHW070121230526
45472CB00004B/1367